Poetry Comics

Poetry Comics

an animated anthology

Dave Morice

T&W Books

New York

Poetry Comics: An Animated Anthology

Library of Congress Cataloging-in-Publication Data

Morice, Dave, 1946–
    Poetry comics : an animated anthology / by Dave Morice.
      p. cm.
    ISBN 0-915924-87-0
    1. English poetry--Comic books, strips, etc. 2. American poetry--Comic books, strips, etc. I. Title.

    PN6727 M673 P64 2002
    741.5'973--dc21

                                                    2002029108

Teachers & Writers Collaborative
5 Union Square West
New York, NY 10003

Cover drawing of William Shakespeare: Dave Morice
Design: Christina Davis and Christopher Edgar

Printed by Thomson-Shore, Dexter, MI. First printing.

Acknowledgments

This book is dedicated to Richard Carlin, Chris Edgar, Joe the Giraffe, and Billy the Hobo Bee.

Thanks to Christina Davis for her work on the cartoons. Thanks to James Stone, Jack Hathaway, Sam Offutt, Nate Haywood, and Danny Morice for their suggestions on the book. Thanks to Gillian Kane for her fact checking and proofreading. Thanks for a variety of reasons to Tom Disch, Bill Zavatsky, Ron Padgett, John Birkbeck, Corinne Joslyn, Jim Denigan, Mark Isham, Steve Schooley, Diane DeBok, Delbert Stevens, Alexander Stevens, and Zobeida Rodriguez.

"Some Trees," from *Some Trees* by John Ashbery. Copyright © 1956 by John Ashbery. Reprinted by permission of Georges Borchardt, Inc. "Harlem" by Langston Hughes. From *The Collected Poems of Langston Hughes* by Langston Hughes, copyright © 1994 by the Estate of Langston Hughes. Used by permission of Alfred A. Knopf, a division of Random House, Inc. Note that in *Poetry Comics* we have followed the practice of referring to "Harlem" as *Montage of a Dream Deferred*, the larger series poem of which "Harlem" is a part. "In a Station of the Metro" by Ezra Pound, from *Personae*, copyright © 1926 by Ezra Pound. Reprinted by permission of New Directions Publishing Corp. "Poetry" by Marianne Moore. Reprinted with the permission of Scribner, an imprint of Simon & Schuster Adult Publishing Group, from *Collected Poems of Marianne Moore* by Marianne Moore. Copyright © 1935 by Marianne Moore; copyright renewed © 1963 by Marianne Moore and T. S. Eliot. Note that "Ten Commandments of Modern Poetry" by Walt Whitman and "Modern Poetry Romance" by Emily Dickinson are facetious titles, and can only be found in this volume. In addition, Morice's version of T. S. Eliot's "The Love Song of J. Alfred Prufrock" is a conflation of many different elements from the poem; it is, indeed, not what he meant at all.

Teachers & Writers programs are made possible in part by grants from the New York City Department of Cultural Affairs and the National Endowment for the Arts, and with public funds from the New York State Council on the Arts, a State Agency. Teachers & Writers Collaborative is also grateful for support from the following foundations and corporations: AKC Fund, Axe-Houghton Foundation, The David and Minnie Berk Foundation, Bronx Borough President and City Council, The Bydale Foundation, The Cerimon Fund, Chelsea Austin Foundation, The Saul Z. and Amy S. Cohen Family Foundation, Consolidated Edison, E.H.A. Foundation, Fleet Bank, The Janet Stone Jones Foundation, Low Wood Fund, Inc., Manhattan City Council Delegation, M & O Foundation, Morgan Stanley Dean Witter Foundation, NBC, New York Community Trust (Van Lier Fund), New York Times Company Foundation, Henry Nias Foundation, North Star Fund, The Open Society Institute, Queens Borough President and City Council, Joshua Ringel Memorial Fund, Maurice R. Robinson Fund, Rush Philanthropic Arts Foundation, St. Ann's School, The Scheide Fund, The Scherman Foundation, Verizon Foundation, and the Wendling Foundation. T&W's 30th-Anniversary Endowed Residencies are supported by Marvin Hoffman and Rosellen Brown, the New World Foundation, Steven Schrader, Alison Wylegala (in memory of Sergio Guerrero), John Gilman (in memory of June Baker), and anonymous donors.

Contents

Preface
The Origin of Poetry Comics   xii

William Shakespeare
Sonnet 18   1
Sonnet 130   8
Full Fathom Five   9

Thomas Wyatt
They Flee from Me   13

George Peele
Hot Sun, Cool Fire   17

Ben Jonson
Song: To Celia (II)   21

Robert Herrick
To the Virgins, to Make Much of Time   25

Thomas Carew
A Song   29

John Dryden
Mac Flecknoe (excerpt)   33

William Blake
The Sick Rose   34
Auguries of Innocence (excerpt)   35

William Wordsworth
She Dwelt Among the Untrodden Ways (excerpt)   36
I Wandered Lonely As a Cloud   37

Percy Bysshe Shelley
Adonais (excerpt)   40

John Keats
On First Looking into Chapman's Homer (excerpt)   41
This Living Hand   42

Alfred, Lord Tennyson
The Eagle   43

Edgar Allan Poe
The Raven   44

Robert Browning
My Last Duchess (excerpt)   63
Fra Lippo Lippi (excerpt)   64

Walt Whitman
"Ten Commandments of Modern Poetry"   70
Leaves of Grass (excerpt)   71

Dante Gabriel Rossetti
The Woodspurge   77

Emily Dickinson
Poem 441   79
Poem 288   80
Poem 303   81
"Modern Poetry Romance"   82

Lewis Carroll
Jabberwocky   86

Ezra Pound
In a Station of the Metro   87

Joyce Kilmer
Trees   88

Marianne Moore
Poetry   89

T. S. Eliot
The Love Song of J. Alfred Prufrock (excerpt)   92
The Hollow Men   100

Langston Hughes
Montage of a Dream Deferred (excerpt)   101

Dylan Thomas
Fern Hill   104

Allen Ginsberg
Howl (excerpt)   105

John Ashbery
Some Trees   111

Appendix
How to Make Poetry Comics   114

Preface
The Origin of Poetry Comics

When did poetry comics begin? In the Neolithic era, the inhabitants of caves in Lascaux, France, and other places painted pictures on the walls of their caves. Around these pictures, they made marks that have been interpreted as fertility symbols, good-luck charms, or magic words. In these early combinations of words and pictures, the paleontologists of language might be reading the very first poetry comics.

At the dawn of written language, Egyptian hieroglyphics and Chinese pictographs simplified visual images to make symbols for verbal concepts. The development of alphabets further abstracted the shapes of letters from their pictorial origins. Linguistic concepts evolved through the transformation of oral to visual representation of words that signify human concepts.

Down through the centuries, writers and artists have produced endless examples of illustrated writings. Consider the illuminated manuscripts of the Middle Ages; Aesop's fables accompanied by woodcuts; William Blake's fusion of art, poetry, and graphic design in *Songs of Innocence, Songs of Experience*; and Lewis Carroll's *Alice in Wonderland*, as famous for John Tenniel's drawings as for the story itself.

Today, the word *cartoon* conjures up visions of Spiderman, Bugs Bunny, Goofy, Batman—everything from a host of Saturday morning animations to a horde of Sunday morning newspaper comics. But *cartoon* originally meant "a full-size preliminary sketch of a design or picture to be copied in a fresco, tapestry, etc." When people refer to Leonardo's "cartoons," therefore, they don't mean that da Vinci drew comic strips.

Comic strips evolved out of European picture stories, which included drawings in sequence, balloons filled with dialogue, and caricature drawings. They appeared in a wide range of publications, from children's books to newspapers. Popular magazines such as Britain's *Punch* published cartoons poking fun at the foibles of the Victorian Age. Indeed, before the days of photo-illustration, editors relied heavily on ink drawings to accompany their texts.

P. F. Outcault's *The Yellow Kid*, published in the United States in the 1890s, is considered by most authorities to be the first real comic strip. On October 18, 1896, it depicted a humorous situation involving a conversation between its lead character the Yellow Kid and a parrot. The dialogue between the two was a necessary part of the joke. In previous cartoon-like strips, the panel drawings were self-explanatory, and the words were merely embellishments. In *The Yellow Kid*, for the first time in history, words and pictures worked in unison to tell the story. By the turn of the century, most cartoons had adopted this approach.

In the Golden Age of 1900–1930, the Sunday humor sections of the more prosperous papers printed full-page color comic strips of Outcault's *Buster Brown*, Winsor McCay's *Little Nemo*, and fifteen or twenty more pages of "funnies." In 1906 the Hearst papers introduced black-and-white strips in the dailies, a format that made it possible for smaller papers to run comic strips.

Around this time literary magazines were beginning to take root—*The Yellow Book* (no relation to *The Yellow Kid* above), *Poetry, Contact,* and the experimental art and literature magazine, *Blast.* The manner in which these journals merged visual art and writing, as well as their slender and ephemeral format (so unlike Victorian tomes), had a great influence on comic books as we now know them.

In the early twentieth century, comic books similarly proliferated. Publishers reprinted newspaper comics in hard- and soft-cover books, constantly trying different formats. Today, DC, Marvel, Gold Key, Archie, and other companies carry on the tradition and do a huge business. Since the 1960s, there has also been an "underground comix" movement. Like the editors of little magazines, comix artists and publishers have full control over their work. They decide on format, printing, distribution, and all other technical details and costs.

Given this rich tradition, it is odd that famous poems have only rarely appeared as cartoon dialogue. In his *Famous Poems Illustrated*, James Thurber took classic bad verse and drew cartoons to accompany it. More recently, *Mad* Magazine printed its own parodies of such classics as Edgar Allan Poe's *The Raven.*

My book is based on the idea that the poem-cartoon combination is quite natural. It evolves from the close relationship that words and pictures have always had. Poetry and cartoonery are both art forms. Together, they can only enrich each other.

—*Dave Morice*

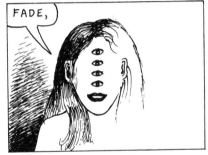

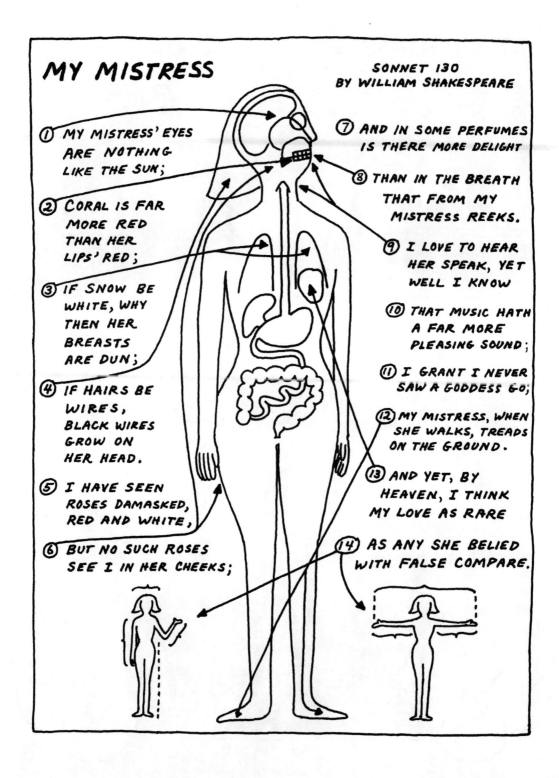

FROM "THE TEMPEST" BY WILLIAM SHAKESPEARE

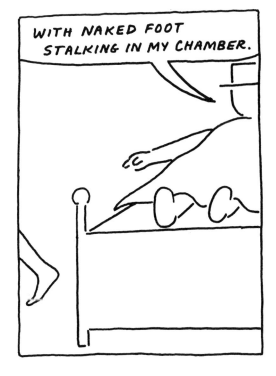

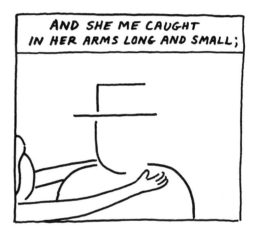

END

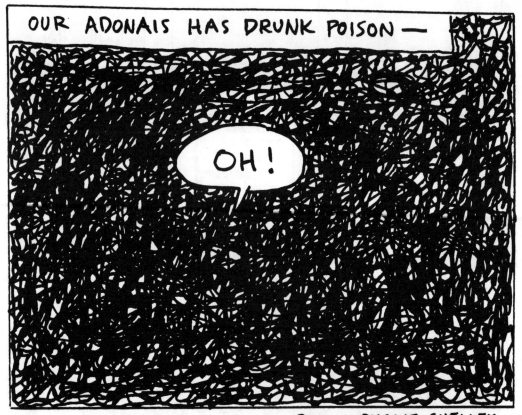

PERCY BYSSHE SHELLEY

"MUCH HAVE I TRAVELED IN THE REALMS OF GOLD"

JOHN KEATS

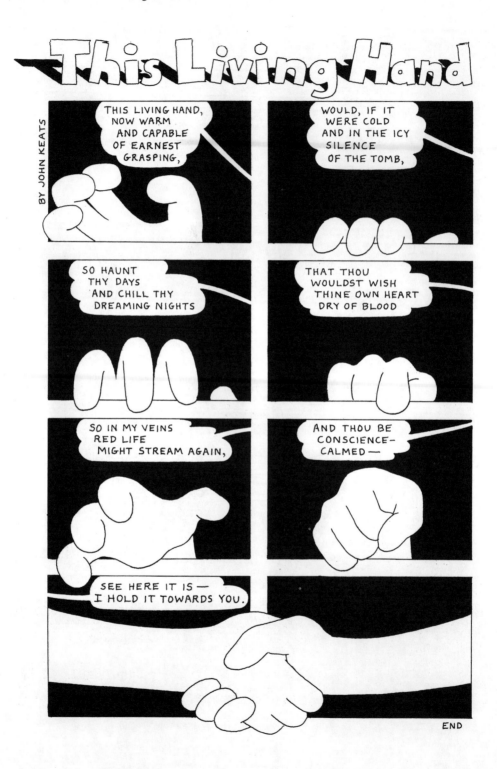

THE EAGLE

HE CLASPS THE CRAG WITH CROOKED HANDS;

BY ALFRED, LORD TENNYSON

CLOSE TO THE SUN IN LONELY LANDS,

RINGED WITH THE AZURE WORLD, HE STANDS.

THE WRINKLED SEA BENEATH HIM CRAWLS;

HE WATCHES FROM HIS MOUNTAIN WALLS,

AND LIKE

A THUNDERBOLT

HE

FALLS.

END

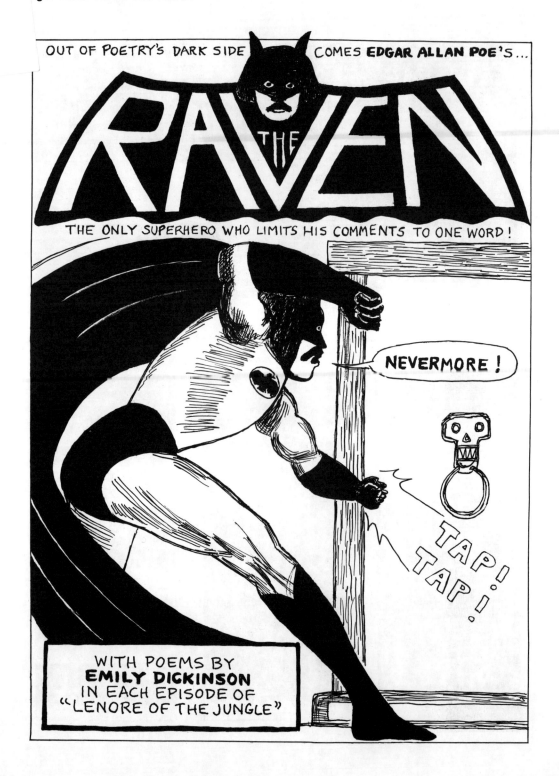

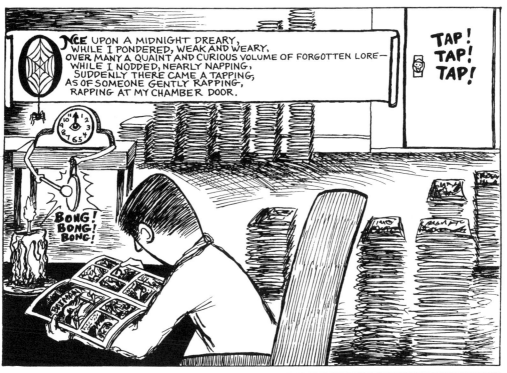

AND THE SILKEN, SAD, UNCERTAIN RUSTLING OF EACH PURPLE CURTAIN THRILLED ME—

FILLED ME WITH FANTASTIC TERRORS NEVER FELT BEFORE;

SO THAT NOW, TO STILL THE BEATING OF MY HEART,

I STOOD REPEATING

'TIS SOME VISITER ENTREATING ENTRANCE AT MY CHAMBER DOOR—

SOME LATE VISITER ENTREATING ENTRANCE AT MY CHAMBER DOOR;—

THIS IT IS AND NOTHING MORE.

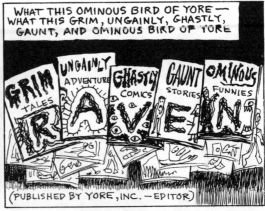

THIS I SAT ENGAGED IN GUESSING, BUT NO SYLLABLE EXPRESSING

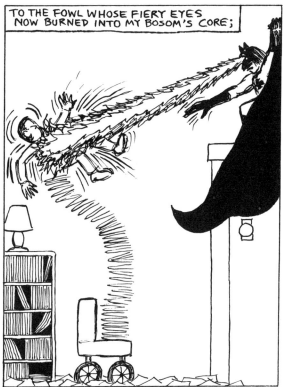

TO THE FOWL WHOSE FIERY EYES NOW BURNED INTO MY BOSOM'S CORE;

THIS AND MORE I SAT DIVINING, WITH MY HEAD AT EASE RECLINING ON THE CUSHION'S VELVET LINING THAT THE LAMP-LIGHT GLOATED O'ER,

BUT WHOSE VELVET-VIOLET LINING WITH THE LAMP-LIGHT GLOATING O'ER, *SHE* SHALL PASS, AH, NEVERMORE!

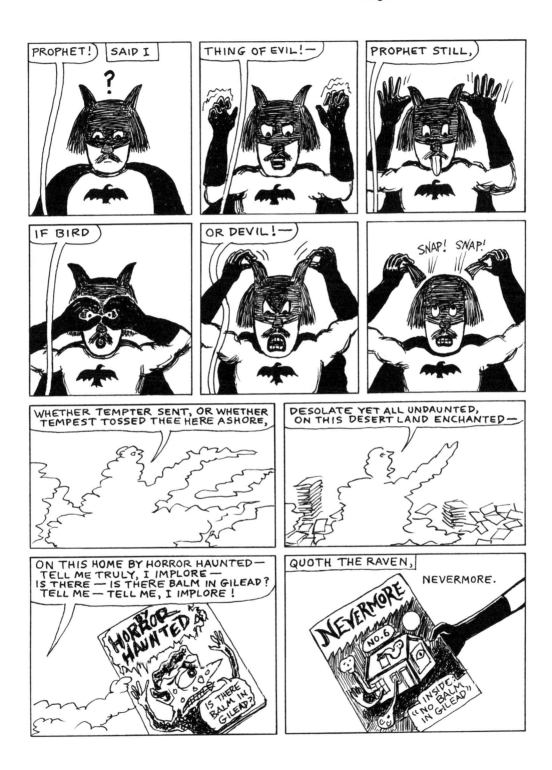

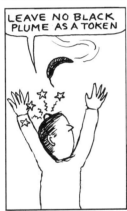

AND THE RAVEN, NEVER FLITTING,

STILL IS SITTING, *STILL* IS SITTING

ON THE PALLID BUST OF PALLAS

JUST ABOVE MY CHAMBER DOOR;

POETRY COMICS

THE RAVEN

AND HIS EYES HAVE ALL THE SEEMING OF A DEMON'S THAT IS DREAMING,

POETRY COMICS

AND THE LAMP-LIGHT O'ER HIM STREAMING THROWS HIS SHADOW ON THE FLOOR;

AND MY SOUL FROM OUT THAT SHADOW THAT LIES FLOATING ON THE FLOOR SHALL BE LIFTED—

NEVERMORE!

END

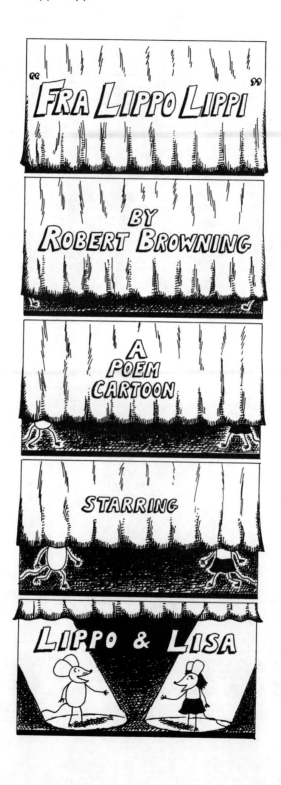

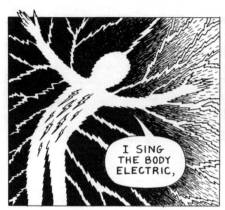

END

END

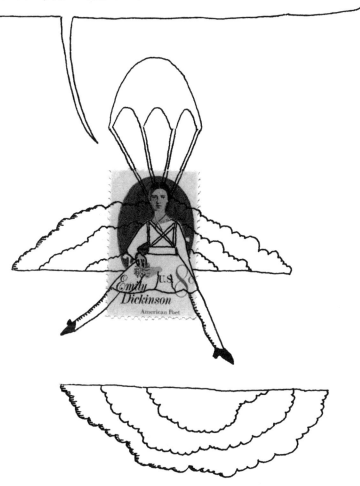

JABBERWOCKY

BY LEWIS CARROLL

'Twas brillig,

And the slithy toves

Did gyre and gimble

In the wabe:

All mimsy were

The borogoves,

And the mome raths

Outgrabe.

"Beware the Jabberwock, my son!

The jaws that bite, the claws that catch!

Beware the Jubjub bird, and shun

The frumious Bandersnatch!"

He took his vorpal sword in hand:

Long time the manxome foe he sought—

So rested he by the Tumtum tree,

And stood awhile in thought.

And, as in uffish thought he stood,

The Jabberwock, with eyes of flame,

Came whiffling through the tulgey wood,

And burbled as it came!

One, two! One, two! And through and through

The vorpal blade went snicker-snack!

He left it dead, and with its head

He went galumphing back.

"And hast thou slain the Jabberwock?

Come to my arms, my beamish boy!

O frabjous day! Callooh! Callay!"

He chortled in his joy.

'Twas brillig, and the slithy toves

Did gyre and gimble in the wabe:

All mimsy were the borogoves,

And the mome raths outgrabe.

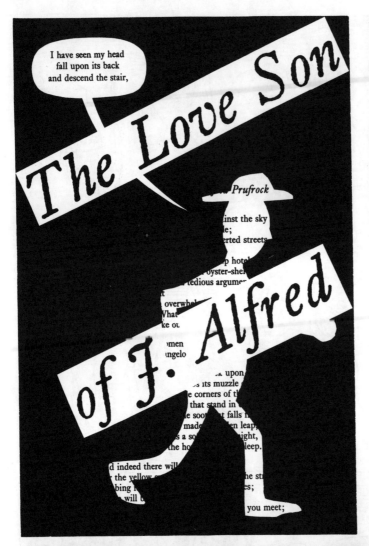

After

The Love Song of J. Alfred Prufrock

By

THOMAS STEARNS ELIOT

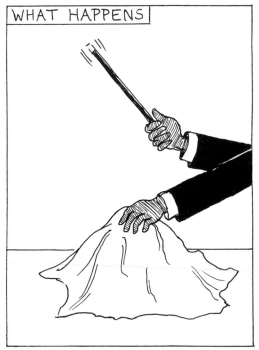

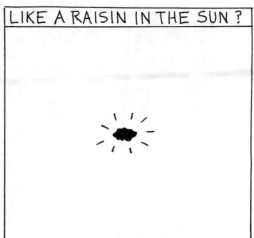

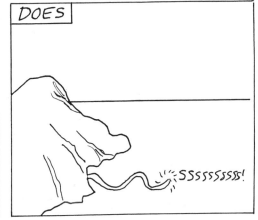

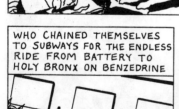

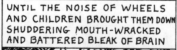

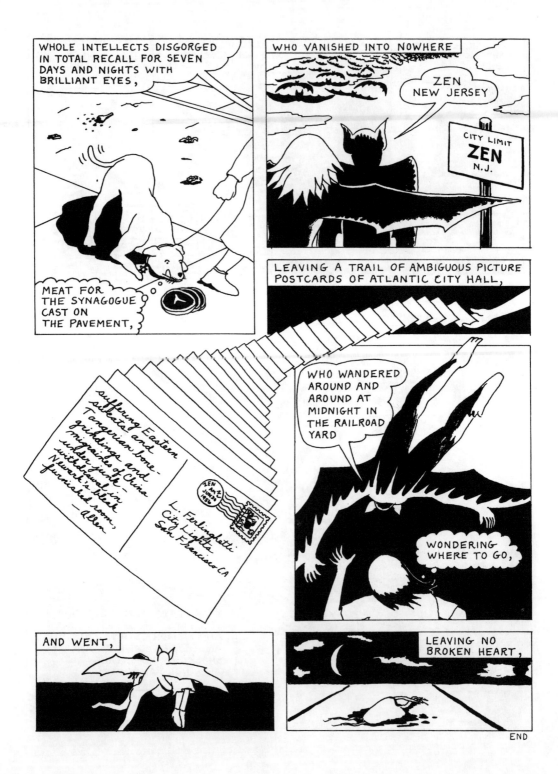

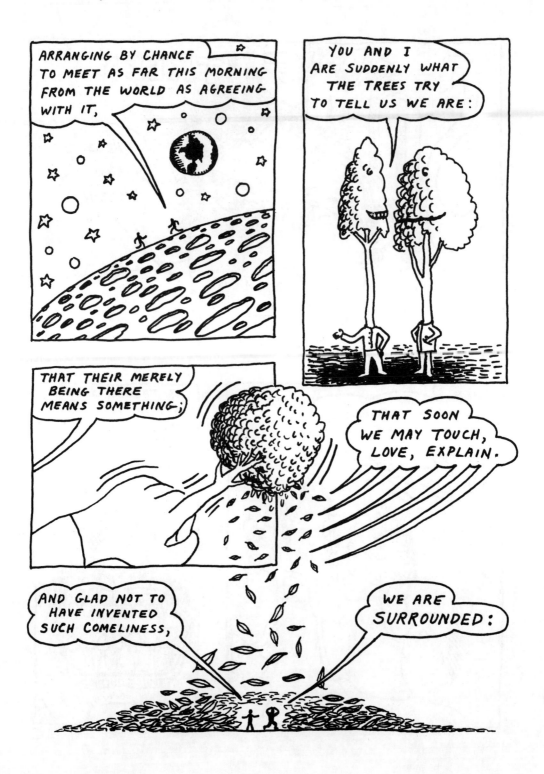

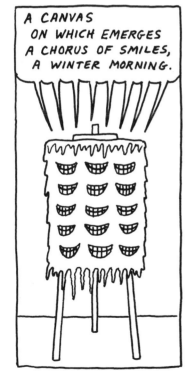

Appendix
How to Make Poetry Comics

Step 1   Choosing Cartoon Formats and Devices

One of the best ways to start making poetry comics is to use the cartoon format. Thanks to comic books and newspaper funnies, most of us are already familiar with the majority of cartoon devices. The following list of commonly used cartoon forms will help you recall the basic elements of the art form. Though some of it may seem to be fairly basic knowledge, it helps to have these terms and definitions handy.

CARTOON PANELS: The **cartoon panel** (see Fig. 1) is the basic building block of cartoon strips and comic books. It is usually rectangular or square, though it can be any shape. It is the "canvas" on which the drawings and words appear. It can operate as a self-contained unit or as part of a larger cartoon strip.

BALLOONS AND BOXES: The cartoon panel uses the following devices to tell a story. When characters speak, their words are put in **speech balloons** (see Fig. 1). The other characters "hear" these, and the reader reads them. Some cartoonists prefer to put the character's words in free space and then draw a short line from the words to the speaker. This device is known as a **free space word**. When characters think, however, their words appear in **thought balloons**. These balloons indicate that other characters cannot hear the words that appear in them. Information that is necessary to the narration—such as, stage directions, moods, time changes—is placed in a **story box**.

CARTOON STRIPS: The **cartoon strip** (see Fig. 2) is a row of cartoon panels, usually three or four that span across the page. Like the cartoon panel, the strip can present a self-contained episode of a continuing story (such as *Dick Tracy* or *Mary Worth*) or it can be part of a more comprehensive comic page (such as, the *Donald Duck* or *Superman* comics).

COMIC PAGES: The **comic page** (see Fig. 3) contains the panels in a specific arrangement—for example, three rows featuring two panels in each row. Most often the page measures 8" x 10" and is read from left to right and top to bottom. The comic page can contain a complete story, part of a story (as in many comic books), or several one-panel or one-strip cartoons.

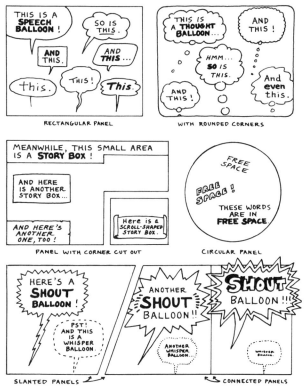

Fig. 1
Cartoon Panels
and Boxes

Fig. 2
Cartoon Strips

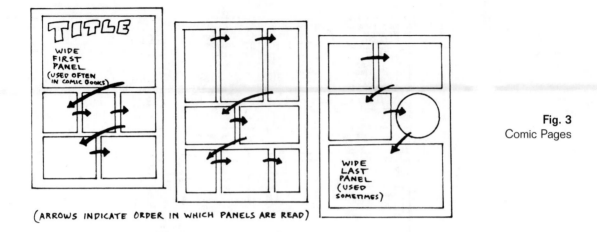

Fig. 3
Comic Pages

(ARROWS INDICATE ORDER IN WHICH PANELS ARE READ)

Step 2   Drawing the Cartoons

After reviewing the fundamental cartoon formats, the next step is to consider the kind of character (or cast of characters) you would like to draw. Superheroes, funny animals, soldiers, monsters, and detectives are just some of the figures featured in contemporary comics. A single page from the daily funnies will suffice to demonstrate the range of possibilities. In this atmosphere of discovery, ideas abound.

Don't be deterred if you feel you lack "artistic ability" or think you can't even draw a straight line. You don't have to be Michelangelo. The twentieth century has shown that traditions are limiting. Great cartoons, like great artworks, don't have to follow the rules. In a comic strip, even a stick figure can speak profoundly.

Step 3   Combining Poems and Cartoons

In moving from poem to cartoon, you take a given group of words and create a visual environment around them. This change automatically affects the tone of the poem. The results can be illustrational, satirical, critical, or surreal. Bringing the two art forms together can help you to understand how each one works, and how they can work together. How are cartoons and poems the same? The first answer is often, "They both have words." How are they different? To this many reply, "Cartoons have pictures." But if you pursue this inquiry further, you will discover many subtler relationships.

In poetry comics, the characters play an important role in determining what the words mean. Consider, for example, the line, "Would you like a piece of cheese?" If spoken by two *Modern Poetry Romance* lovers, it might be a flirtatious remark at a wine and cheese party. But if a ferocious cat says it to a cornered mouse, it's probably an ironic threat.

Any poem can be illustrated in an amazing number of forms and styles, with one or more characters. The result can range from literal interpretation to humorous take-off. The Ancient Mariner can be a realistically drawn seaman wizened by the years or a white-bearded version of Popeye. Simply go in the direction your pencil and pen takes you.